TOP COUNTRY HITS
2011-2012

ISBN 978-1-4584-2298-9

HAL•LEONARD®
CORPORATION
7777 W. BLUEMOUND RD. P.O. BOX 13819 MILWAUKEE, WI 53213

Visit Hal Leonard Online at
www.halleonard.com

BAGGAGE CLAIM

Words and Music by MIRANDA LAMBERT
LUKE LAIRD and NATALIE HEMBY

BAREFOOT BLUE JEAN NIGHT

Words and Music by DYLAN ALTMAN,
ERIC PASLAY and TERRY SAWCHUK

CRAZY GIRL

Words and Music by LIZ ROSE
and LEE BRICE

Moderately, with a lilt

Ba - by, why you wan - na cry? __ You real - ly ought - a know that I __
I would - n't last a sin - gle day. __ I'd prob - 'ly just __ fade a - way. __

just have to walk a - way some - times.
With - out __ you, I'd __ lose my mind.

We're gon - na do what lov - ers do. __ We're gon - na have a fight or two, __
Be - fore you ev - er came a - long, __ I was liv - in' life all wrong. __

EASY

Words and Music by KATRINA ELAM
and MICHAEL MOBLEY

Male: We broke up; ___ yeah, it's tough. Most guys would-a been crushed, ___

wast - in' _____ their time won - d'rin where they went wrong. _____

No way, not me. Hey, I'm do - in' just _____

far — as — he — knows.—— It's eas - y go-ing out on Fri-day night. Eas - y ev -'ry time I —— see him out. I can smile, live it up the way a sin-gle girl — does. But what he, what he don't know —— is how hard it is to make it look so eas - y.——

Guitar solo ad lib.

GOD GAVE ME YOU

Words and Music by
DAVE BARNES

I've __ been a walk - ing heart - ache;
There's more __ here than what we're see - ing,

I've __ made a mess of me. __
a di - vine con - spir - a - cy: __

The per - son that I've been late - ly
that you, _____ an an - gel love - ly,

ain't __ who I wan - na be. __ But,
could __ some - how fall for me. __

but you stay __ here __ right __ be - side me
You'll al - ways be love's __ great __ mar - tyr;

gave _ me you. _

HONEY BEE

Words and Music by RHETT AKINS
and BEN HAYSLIP

JUST A KISS

Words and Music by HILLARY SCOTT,
DALLAS DAVIDSON, CHARLES KELLEY
and DAVE HAYWOOD

Moderately slow

Female:
Ly - in' here _ with you _ so close to me, ___ it's hard to fight _ these feel-

-in's when it feels _ so hard to breathe. _ I'm caught up in ___ this mo-

Recorded a half step lower.

IF HEAVEN WASN'T SO FAR AWAY

Words and Music by ROBERT HATCH,
BRETT JONES and DALLAS DAVIDSON

Recorded a half step lower.

LET IT RAIN

Words and Music by DAVID NAIL
and JONATHAN SINGLETON

Moderate Country Ballad

Lyrics:

It's hard to find the per-fect time to say something you know is gon-na change ev'-ry-thing.

down on me. ____ Ev-'ry word, ____ let it hurt ____ e - ven more _

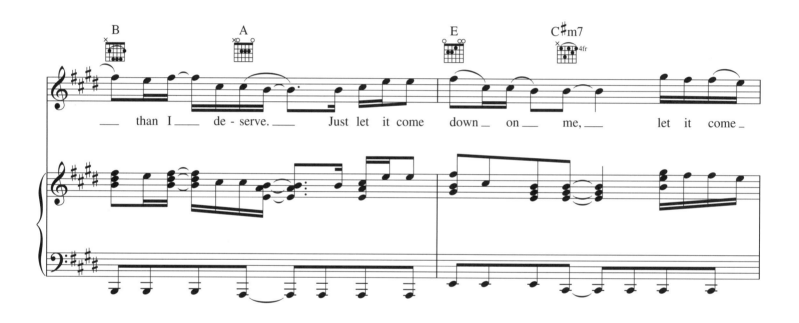

____ than I ____ de - serve. ____ Just let it come down _ on __ me, ___ let it come _

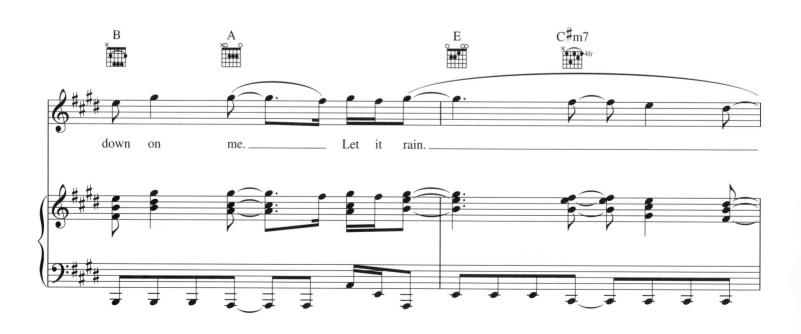

down on me. _____ Let it rain. _____

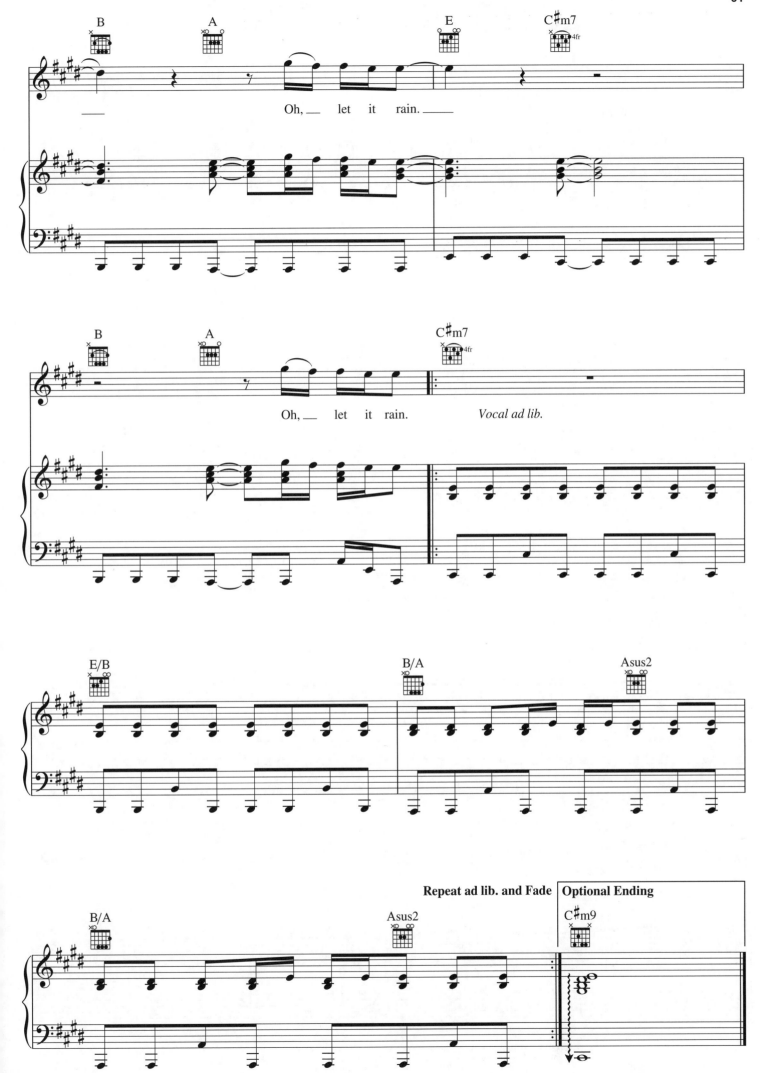

LONG HOT SUMMER

Words and Music by KEITH URBAN
and RICHARD MARX

SPARKS FLY

Words and Music by
TAYLOR SWIFT

The way you move is like a full-on rain-storm and I'm a house of cards. You're the

WE OWNED THE NIGHT

Words and Music by DALLAS DAVIDSON,
CHARLES KELLEY and DAVE HAYWOOD

Tell me, have you ev - er want - ed some - one so much it hurts?

Your lips ___ keep try'n' to speak, but you just can't find the words.

Well, I had this dream once; I held it in my

Recorded a half step higher.

Oh. _____ Oh. _____

Oh. _____

Oh. _____

TAKE A BACK ROAD

Words and Music by RHETT AKINS
and LUKE LAIRD

Sit in that six-lane, backed-up traf-fic; horns are honk-in'. I've _

TATTOOS ON THIS TOWN

Words and Music by NEIL THRASHER,
WENDELL MOBLEY and MICHAEL DULANEY

There's still black _ marks on _ that coun-

TOMORROW

Words and Music by CHRIS YOUNG,
FRANK MYERS and ANTHONY SMITH

*Recorded a half step higher.